1295

# Grover's
# 10 Terrific Ways to Help Our Wonderful World

## By Anna Ross

## Illustrated by Tom Leigh

**On Sesame Street Luis is performed by Emilio Delgado.**

Published in the United States by Random House, Inc.,
New York, and simultaneously in Canada by Random House of
Canada Limited, Toronto, in conjunction with the
Children's Television Workshop.

Library of Congress Cataloging-in-Publication Data
Ross, Anna.
Grover's 10 terrific ways to help our wonderful world / by Anna Ross ; illustrated by Tom Leigh.
p.     cm. — (A Random House pictureback)
Published in conjunction with the Children's Television Workshop.
Summary: Grover describes ten ways to help the world,
from planting trees to recycling trash.
ISBN 0-679-81384-5 (trade) — ISBN 0-679-91384-X (lib. bdg.)
[1. Environmental protection—Fiction.   2. Recycling (Waste)—
Fiction.]   I. Leigh, Tom. ill.   II. Children's Television
Workshop.   III. Title.
PZ7.R71962Gr   1992
[E]—dc20                                                        91-11095
Manufactured in the United States of America

E ROS

11  12  13  14  15  16  17  18  19  20

## Random House 🏠 New York

Hello, everybody!
The world is such a wonderful place!

The world is our home.
The mountains and deserts,
the rivers and lakes belong
to all of us.

The world gives us everything we need to live.
It gives us food to eat and water to drink
and air to breathe.

The world gives us snow
and sunshine and rain!

The world takes care of us, so
we must take care of the world.
Oh, I know we can do it!

I, Grover the World Ranger,
will tell you ten terrific ways
to help our wonderful world.

People and animals and plants
all need one another. So…

1
PLANT A TREE.

PROTECT OUR ANIMAL FRIENDS.

Instead of buying
new things or
throwing old things away...

3

FIX
BROKEN THINGS.

DO NOT WASTE WATER.

Bert turns off the faucet instead of running the water while he brushes his teeth.

Ernie keeps water nice and
cold in the refrigerator
instead of letting the water
run until it's cold enough.

**DO NOT WASTE ENERGY.**

Telly turns off the TV
when his program is over.

The Count turns off the lights
when he leaves the room.

Betty Lou uses cold water instead of hot water
whenever she can. It takes energy to heat water.

Cookie Monster closes the
refrigerator door quickly so
the cold air can't get out.
It takes energy to cool air.

DO NOT WASTE THINGS THAT CAN BE USED ANOTHER WAY.

6

Ernie plants his seeds
in empty milk cartons.
When the plants are big enough,
he'll put them in the window box.

Bert sorts his brown buttons and precious
paper clips into an old egg carton.

Grouches are great at making treasures
out of trash!

1 GIVE OUTGROWN THINGS TO SOMEONE SMALLER.

When Snuffy's sweaters get too small,
he gives them to his little sister, Alice.

When Elmo learns to ride a two-wheeler,
he will give his tricycle to Baby Natasha.

8 CHOOSE THINGS THAT CAN BE USED OVER AND OVER AGAIN.

Prairie Dawn takes her lunch
in a lunchbox instead of
in a plastic bag.

Bert uses a sponge
instead of a paper towel
to clean up.

Big Bird takes
his own shopping bag
to the supermarket
instead of getting
a new bag every time.

PICK UP LITTER.

My friends and I take bottles and cans to places
where they can be picked up and recycled

We tie up newspapers in bundles and put them out at the curb so the recycling truck can pick them up. Old paper can be recycled to make new paper.

Oh, I am so happy!
There is so much we can do
to help our wonderful world!

1. PLANT A TREE.
2. PROTECT OUR ANIMAL FRIENDS.
3. FIX BROKEN THINGS.
4. DO NOT WASTE WATER.
5. DO NOT WASTE ENERGY.
6. DO NOT WASTE THINGS THAT CAN BE USED ANOTHER WAY.
7. GIVE OUTGROWN THINGS TO SOMEONE SMALLER.
8. CHOOSE THINGS THAT CAN BE USED OVER AND OVER AGAIN.
9. PICK UP LITTER.
10. RECYCLE TRASH.